SOUTHERN
STEAM
ON THE ISLE OF WIGHT

TONY FAIRCLOUGH AND **ALAN WILLS**

D. BRADFORD BARTON LIMITED

Frontispiece: The 1.30 p.m. Ryde (Pier Head) to Cowes threads the luxuriant vegetation half a mile west of Haven Street behind No. 17 *Seaview* on 7 August 1965.

[T. P. Cooper]

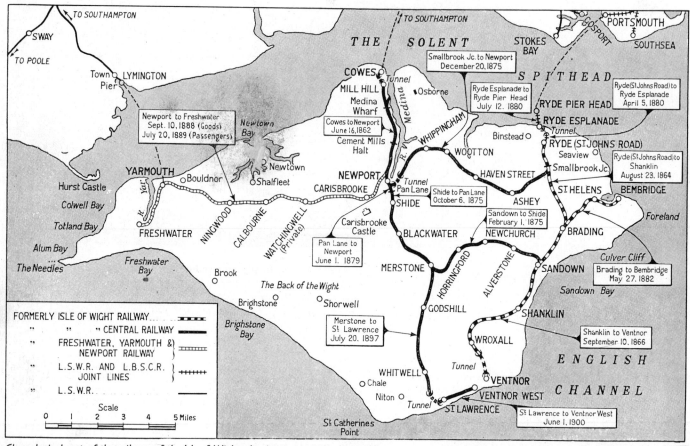

Chronological map of the railways of the Isle of Wight, showing pre-grouping ownerships

Reproduced by courtesy of *The Railway Magazine*

© *copyright D. Bradford Barton Ltd 1975*   *ISBN 0 85153 228 4*

printed in Great Britain by Thomson Litho Ltd, East Kilbride, Scotland

for the publisher

D. BRADFORD BARTON LTD · Trethellan House · Truro · Cornwall · England

introduction

The story of railway development on the Isle of Wight can be taken, on a miniature scale, as representative of the growth of railways in Britain. The Island, twenty miles long from east to west and thirteen from north to south, was gripped by the Railway Mania of 1845, but it was not until 1862 that trains first rattled along the line between Cowes and Newport. There then followed the usual Victorian pattern of independent planning and construction of lines between centres of importance. In all, seven companies were involved in the promotion of the 45 route miles on the Island, but, as on the mainland, several of the smaller companies merged into larger concerns in order to operate the traffic in a more economical manner.

The year 1923 was a landmark in the Island's railway history, as it was elsewhere in Britain. The newly-formed Southern Railway became responsible for the Isle of Wight and the new management was not impressed with the situation which it had inherited. From the enthusiasts' viewpoint, the decision of the S.R. to transfer redundant '02' 0-4-4Ts to replace the miscellaneous collection of tanks on the Island was a stroke of genius. Although already over thirty years old, these splendid little Adams engines, carrying names of local interest, became the epitome of Isle of Wight working. Furthermore they remained in command until the cessation of steam working at the close of 1966, making the transition to National ownership with little more than a change of livery.

Although the lines played a tremendous part in the growth of the holiday trade, winter business was always slack and after the Island's railways began losing money, the first closures came in 1952. Dr Beeching proposed the complete abandonment of railways on Wight, but fortunately the Ryde to Shanklin line was salvaged to become the only electrified route on the Island, but, true to tradition, the 'new' rolling stock was thirty-year-old ex-London Underground trains, converted to run on the standard Southern third-rail system. But steam can still be seen and heard, as the members of the Wight Locomotive Society operate a $1\frac{1}{2}$ mile stretch of line from Haven Street to Wootton. They are building up a representative collection of stock at Haven Street, with '02' No. 24 *Calbourne* having pride of place as its principal motive power.

The driver of No. 33 *Bembridge* poses for the cameraman in the bright summer sunshine at Ryde (Pier Head) in 1965. The Island engines were numbered on a separate list with the prefix 'W' to distinguish them from the mainland engines. This letter appeared on the cast number plates on the rear of the bunker and was used in official records, but was not painted with the prominently displayed locomotive number on the side of the bunker from 1931 onwards.

[T. P. Cooper]

Nos. 24 *Calbourne* and 14 *Fishbourne* have both been specially cleaned for working the L.C.G.B. 'Vectis Farewell' Rail Tour on 3 October 1965. Several enthusiasts are taking the chance of having a word with the crew before setting out from the Pier Head station.   [T. P. Cooper]

No. 14 *Fishbourne*, seen in mourning at Ryde (Esplanade) late on 31 December 1966, at the head of the last B.R. steam train to run on the Isle of Wight. The first train ran from Cowes to Newport on 16 June 1862, so steam power exceeded its century innings on the Island by some four years.   [T. P. Cooper]

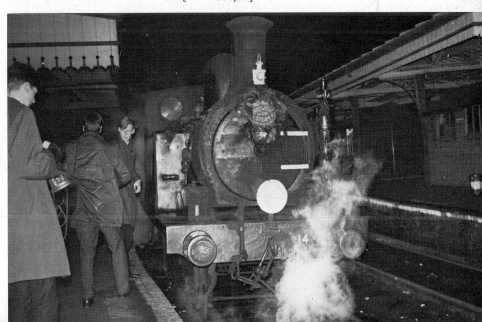

Ryde (Pier Head) station on a busy summer Saturday, 6 June 1964. No. 16 *Ventnor* steams away from the platform, with the pier tramway showing prominently on its separate structure in the foreground. This system, first worked by horse traction on 29 August 1864, was built to provide a service along the 1704-foot pier for the passengers arriving by ferry from Portsmouth. Siemens electric traction was introduced in 1886, to be replaced by the two petrol driven Drewry railcars in 1927 which maintained the service until the closure of the tramway in January, 1969.

[W. L. Underhay]

Adams '02' 0-4-4T No. 16 *Ventnor* waits in No. 1 Platform at Ryde (Pier Head) as No. 27 *Merstone* takes water in Platform 2, June 1966. The track along the pier to the terminus was opened to traffic on 12 July 1880, the line from St. John's Road having been sponsored jointly by the L.S.W.R. and L.B.S.C.R. companies in the expectation of increased traffic to the Island resorts via their main line routes from London to Portsmouth. The station was modernised and enlarged in 1933 as the attractions of the Island encouraged the growth of the tourist trade.

[T. P. Cooper]

Smoke and steam trail across the waters of Spithead as No. 28 *Ashey* approaches the Esplanade station at Ryde on 17 September 1966, the last day of steam working on the pier. The paddle steamer *Ryde* prepares for its return trip to Portsmouth.   [A. E. Bennett]

Ryde (Esplanade) station, built partly on the land with the remainder extending out over the sea, was opened to traffic on 5 April 1880 after years of negotiation and dispute. The idea of a line from St. John's Road to the pier was first proposed as early as 1865, but the difficulties of running a line through the built-up areas of Ryde held up the work until the problem was solved by the construction of a tunnel, 391 yards long, under part of the town. No. 21 *Sandown* leaves for Pier Head on 19 June 1965.   [M. J. Fox]

No. 35 *Freshwater* rumbles along the pier towards Ryde (Esplanade) on 11 August 1966.   [T. P. Cooper]

August 1939 at Ryde (Esplanade). 'E1' 0-6-0T No. 2 *Yarmouth* heads a down Ventnor train, with an I.W.C.R. rail motor coach in the lead.
[C. G. Woodnutt]

No. 14 *Fishbourne* pulls out of St. John's Road on 19 June 1965. Twenty-one of these useful little engines were transferred to the Island shortly after Grouping, followed by a further two in the post war years.　　　　　[M. J. Fox]

St. John's Road was the original terminus at Ryde, marking the northern end of the first section of track which was opened on 23 August 1864 and extended as far as Shanklin, seven miles to the south. No. 21 *Sandown* powers a Ventnor train over a century later on 19 June 1965.　　　　[M. J. Fox]　　13

No. 27 *Merstone* leaves Ryde behind as it passes the Mound, a quarter of a mile south of St. John's Road station, in the summer of 1966. Southbound trains from Ryde were usually hauled chimney-first by the Adams tanks.

[T. P. Cooper]

The 7.40 a.m. Saturday train from Pier Head to Shanklin was often double headed. These two views, taken near Smallbrook Junction in the summer of 1966 show Nos. 17 *Seaview* and 31 *Chale* in the upper study, with No. 31 again, piloting No. 27 *Merstone* in the lower.

[T. P. Cooper]

Nos. 21 *Sandown* and
and 18 *Ningwood*
approach Smallbrook
Junction with the
7.40 a.m. from Pier
Head on 12 June 1965.
Usually the driver of the
pilot engine controlled
the brake when trains
were double headed.
[A. E. Bennett]

No. 21, November 1956. [A. E. Bennett]

The driver has given No. 22 *Brading* full regulator as he tackles the climb to Smallbrook Junction with the 3.25 p.m. from Pier Head on 14 June 1963. Six bogies (150 tons), was the usual permitted maximum for an '02' on the sharply graded Island lines.

[P. Paye]

A Ventnor to Ryde train rolls past Smallbrook Junction box behind No. 20 *Shanklin* on 4 September 1965. [D. M. Cox]

Signalman Vic Hayles of Smallbrook Junction holds out the tablet for the driver of a Ventnor train, 31 July 1965. Country signalmen were loyal and efficient railwaymen and were often great 'characters'. Many, declared redundant, have left the service, leaving it the poorer. [A. E. Bennett]

The box at Smallbrook Junction, nearly three miles south of Pier Head, controlled the junction of the routes from Ryde to Ventnor and Newport. During the winter months the box was closed and the tracks used as two single line sections, but during the summer season, heavily laden trains streamed in both directions. The driver of No. 27 (minus its *Merstone* nameplates) prepares to take the tablet for the Smallbrook-Brading single line, June 1966.

[G. D. King]

The scoured buffers of No. 19 *Osborne* were nothing out of the ordinary in October 1937, back in the days when passenger engines were well maintained as a matter of course. The Ryde to Ventnor train is passing Truckells, about one mile south of Smallbrook Junction.

[C. G. Woodnutt]

A down train jogs through the delightful countryside south of Smallbrook Junction behind No. 31 *Chale* in the summer of 1966. This engine is carrying a Drummond boiler, easily recognisable by the safety valves mounted on the dome instead of above the firebox as on the Adams design of boiler.

[T. P. Cooper]

Twenty nine years later, in the summer of 1966, another down train passes the same spot. The engine is so grimy that its number is indecipherable, a sad commentary on the declining standard of railway maintenance.

[T. P. Cooper]

A down train arrives at Brading, some five miles from Pier Head, in 1922. The scene shows the sort of assets which the Southern had to take over in 1923. The unnumbered 31-ton 2-4-0T *Wroxall* was supplied to the Isle of Wight Railway by Beyer, Peacock Ltd. (No. 1141) in 1872 and was scrapped by the S.R. as No. 16 in 1933, being the last survivor of its class on the Island.

[T. P. Cooper Collection]

'Terrier' No. 13 *Carisbrooke* at Bembridge on the 'new' turntable which was installed c.1936. The small table, 16 ft. 5 in. long and the only one on the Island, was used to enable engines to run around their trains at the terminus of the line which ran from Brading, 2¾ miles away. After Grouping, there were seven 'A1Xs' at work on the Island.

[C. G. Woodnutt]

No. 20 *Shanklin* has come off
its train at Bembridge and is
seen changing tracks in order
to run around the sto   . This
unorthodox layout was
necessary as there was no
room for any extension of the
track beyond the points as in
conventional trackwork; the
public highway runs
immediately behind the table.

[T. P. Cooper]

Running round completed,
No. 20 now stands at the
head of its train for the return
run to Brading. The two tracks
can be seen converging on
the table behind the rear coach.
The polished metalwork of the
engine denotes a pre-war
scene, in fact 25 April 1937.
The branch was opened to
traffic on 27 May 1882 and
operated under the 'one engine
in steam' principle until 21
September 1953, when all
services were withdrawn.

[T. P. Cooper]

With the Ventnor line signals at clear, No. 33 *Bembridge* has just reached the points at Smallbrook Junction with its down train in August 1965. The Victorian engine and stock had served the Island well for some forty years and were soon to disappear from the scene, replaced by the 4-VEC and 3-TIS sets of refurbished London Transport stock which went into operation on this stretch of line on 20 March 1967.

[T. P. Cooper]

Unusually running chimney-first, No. 14 *Fishbourne* arrives at Brading with an up train, 1938. The vintage locomotive and rolling stock are well matched by the printing and weighing machines standing on the platform under the awning.

[C. G. Woodnutt]

How well the Island '02s' looked in pre-war days when their green livery was cleaned to perfection. The paintwork of No. 19 *Osborne* has been polished with cleaning oil, while the brightwork has been scoured. This engine is fitted with a deep-toned hooter, distinguishable from the more usual Southern whistle by its size. Driver Willis takes a breather as the engine takes water at Brading on Sunday 27 May 1934.

[C. G. Woodnutt]

Plenty of power was available for this short parcels train, seen approaching Brading at Whitefield Woods on 7 August 1965. The engines are Nos. 20 *Shanklin* and 31 *Chale*.   [A. E. Bennett]

No. 35 *Freshwater* leaves Brading with a down train on the up line, due to an earth slip near Sandown, 12 March 1966. Such working required very stringent safety precautions to be strictly observed. A pilotman, wearing his official armband, would hand the driver a 'Wrong Line Ticket' which would have to be handed personally to the signalman at the end of the single-line section. If possible, the pilotman would travel with the driver on the footplate in order to help keep a sharp lookout while on the wrong line.
                                                                                          [T. P. Cooper]

e B.R. lined-black livery of No. 20 *Shanklin* had been thoroughly cleaned before the tank worked the 9.42 a.m.
mney-first from Ventnor to Ryde (Pier Head) on 11 June 1952. The driver is accelerating the six-coach train away
m Sandown station.   [Brian Morrison]

The lines from Newport and Ryde to Ventnor joined at Sandown station, six miles south of Ryde. No. 35 *Freshwater* heads out of
Sandown towards Ventnor with the 4.27 p.m. from Pier Head, 27 September 1963.   [G. D. King]

The 3.27 p.m. Pier Head to Ventnor on the two-mile section between Sandown and Shanklin behind No. 36
Carisbrooke, 27 September 1963.   [G. D. King]

The fireman has built
a good head of
steam as No. 14
...hbourne hammers up
the 1 in 85 out of
...ndown past Los Altos
...rk with a Ventnor
...in, August 1966. The
...tle tank, almost at the
...ose of its long working
...e, is steaming well,
...th the Ramsbottom
...fety valves blowing off
...160 lbs. per sq. in.
...e Sandown signalbox
...clearly visible, perched
...ove the station
...wning.   [T. P. Cooper]

No. 35 *Freshwater*
emerges from Cliff's
Bridge as it storms up
Apse Bank, two
gruelling miles of 1 in
70/190 between Shanklin
and Wroxall, on 8 April
1966.   [A. E. Bennett]

Freshwater is seen on its
return run, passing
under Three Arch Bridge
at the summit of
Apse Bank. The '02s'
were smooth-riding
engines, especially when
running bunker-first
downhill, with the bogie
to act as a guide around
the curves.
    [A. E. Bennett]

Trouble at Shanklin, 27 August 1962. The brakevan is fouling the running line but the breakdown crane is at hand, with '02' No. 28 *Ashey* in attendance to provide motive power.

[A. E. Bennett]

The local Fire Brigade gives a hand at the derailment, supplying water for No. 28 *Ashey*. Engine drivers were responsible for ensuring that their locomotive boilers always held at least the minimum requirement of water and this could become a serious problem when access to the normal supply was restricted.

[A. E. Bennett]

An '02' in Maunsell livery, *circa* 1936. The mainland tanks, at that period, had the number on the side tanks beneath the Company's title, but the Island engines had the nameplate in that position, hence the number on the bunker. No. 15 *Cowes* is in charge of a down train at Sandown.

[C. G. Woodnutt]

The Saturdays-only 7.40 a.m. from Ryde (Pier Head) has arrived at Shanklin, in August 1966 and the pilot, No. 24 *Calbourne,* has cut off from the train engine, No. 27 *Merstone.* The 8½ mile line from Pier Head to Shanklin is all that remains of the B.R. network on the Island, worked by six four-car sets (4-VEC) in the winter augmented by six three-car sets (3-TIS) to form seven-car VECTIS sets in the summer season. These sets are ex-London Transport stock of 1938 vintage, and were chosen because of their easy conversion to third rail working, their low profile which fits the restricted loading gauge and above all their low price which was little more than scrap value. While this rolling stock has little to offer the nostalgic enthusiast, it does mean that trains are still running on the Island.   [T. P. Cooper]

No. 31 *Chale* tackles Apse Bank as
she heads for Ventnor with the
'Tourist', the through train from
Freshwater, 1936.

[C. G. Woodnutt]

The 4.27 p.m. Ryde (Pier Head) to
Ventnor steams under Three Arch
Bridge on Apse Bank behind No.
35 *Freshwater* on 19 September 1963.

[P. Paye]

No. 21 *Sandown* climbs into Wroxall station, ten miles from Pier Head with the 2.28 p.m. from Ryde on 2 July 1961. Originally a halt, the station was enlarged by the S.R. in 1925 and the passing loop was installed to ease traffic congestion during the holiday season.

[D. T. Cobbe]

No. 21 again, seen leaving Wroxall for Ventnor on 31 July 1965. The fireman has been plying his shovel, building up a good fire for the 1 in 88 climb out of the station towards Ventnor. The hotel building, seen on the up platform, once housed the station refreshment room.

[A. E. Bennett]

The Saturday morning peace is shattered by the pair of '02s' barking up the bank past Los Altos Park, Sandown, on 3 July 1965, as No. 16 *Ventnor* and No. 24 *Calbourne* heave the 7.40 a.m. from Pier Head up the 1 in 80. Fortunately No. 24, having been rescued from the scrap heap, has been restored by the Wight Locomotive Society and is now at Haven Street station. The ex-Underground electrics which have replaced the 0-4-4 tanks are efficient carriers of the considerable numbers of visitors who still use the line to Shanklin, but trouble has been experienced with the electrics during periods of heavy snowfall when they could not push themselves through the drifts.

[A. E. Bennett]

No. 35 *Freshwater* waits at Wroxall for the single-line section to Ventnor in August 1965, as another '02' clears the section with an up train.   [T. P. Cooper]

The L.C.G.B. Vectis Farewell Tour makes a photographic stop at Wroxall on Sunday 3 October 1965. No. 14 *Fishbourne* and No. 24 *Calbourne* have been specially cleaned for the trip.   [T. P. Cooper]

A fireman's eye view of the line ahead; No. 36 *Carisbrooke* approaches the Ventnor fixed distant at the entrance of the tunnel in August 1963. The small-boilered '02s' had excellent forward visibility for the crew in spite of the presence of the air reservoir and donkey pump on the fireman's side of the engine.   [P. Paye]

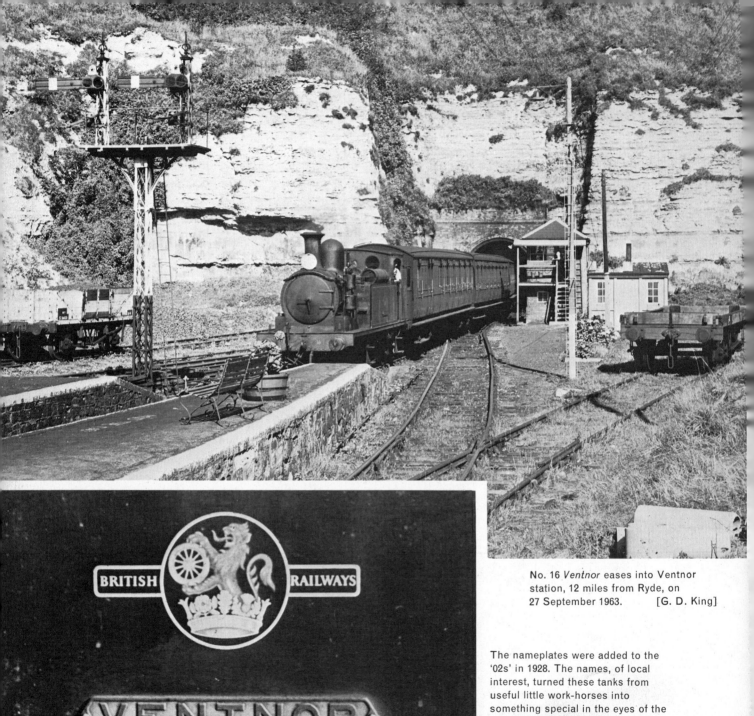

No. 16 *Ventnor* eases into Ventnor
station, 12 miles from Ryde, on
27 September 1963.   [G. D. King]

The nameplates were added to the
'02s' in 1928. The names, of local
interest, turned these tanks from
useful little work-horses into
something special in the eyes of the
travelling public and was a well-
worth-while exercise in
publicity.   [A. E. Bennett]

BRITISH RAILWAYS

VENTNOR

Following a visit to Ryde Works for a general overhaul, No. 17 *Seaview* looks spick-and-span as it emerges from the 1312-yd. tunnel under St. Boniface Downs into the terminus at Ventnor, 9 June 1952. The Island engines never acquired the B.R. smokebox numberplates which were standardised for the majority of mainland engines, but retained neatly-painted numerals on the buffer beam.

[Brian Morrison]

Having run around its train, No. 35 *Freshwater* pulls away from Ventnor on 27 September 1963. The station was built in a deep chalk cutting and several of the caves in the background were used as stores by the local coal merchants.

[G. D. King

A general view of the station at Ventnor, as seen from the Downs above the tunnel, in the summer of 1965, showing the unusual arrangement of the platforms and tracks; if the outer face of the island platform was used, a gangplank had to be placed over intervening track. The length of trains was strictly limited by the position of the points at either end of the station, six bogies and the tank engine being the absolute maximum. The station, the southern terminus of the Isle of Wight Railway, was opened on 10 September 1866.

[T. P. Cooper]

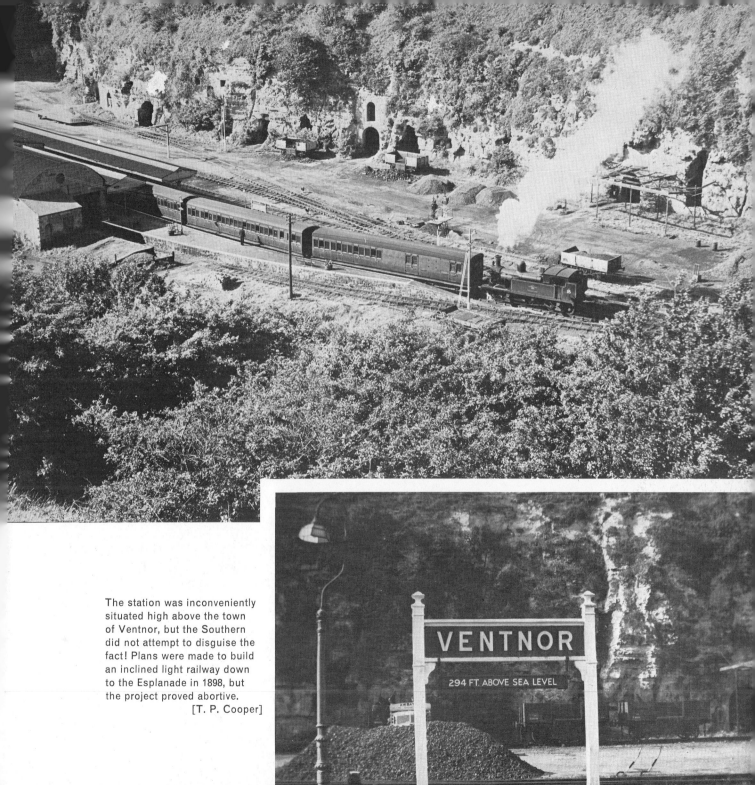

The station was inconveniently situated high above the town of Ventnor, but the Southern did not attempt to disguise the fact! Plans were made to build an inclined light railway down to the Esplanade in 1898, but the project proved abortive.

[T. P. Cooper]

VENTNOR

294 FT. ABOVE SEA LEVEL

No. 27 *Merstone* has run around and is now easing forward on to the stock in the platform. The signalman has the tablet ready for the engine crew to carry up to Wroxall on their return trip to Ryde, 20 May 1956. This engine has a Drummond boiler; these were unpopular with the men who found them more prone to priming when worked hard than the excellent Adams design to be found on the majority of the '02s'.

[A. E. Bennett]

A quiet spring afternoon at Ventnor with No. 14 *Fishbourne* simmering at the head of its train, 30 April 1958. The small holes above the cab spectacles provided some through ventilation for the footplatemen in the small cab of this well-proportioned Adams tank.   [J. R. Besley]

A scene soon to be something from the past. The fireman of No. 14 *Fishbourne* catches the tablet from the Ventnor signalman on 17 April 1966, the last day of working on the Shanklin to Ventnor section of the line which had served the area well for almost 100 years, during which time Ventnor had grown from an obscure village to a prosperous resort of six thousand inhabitants.

[A. E. Bennett]

The 3.42 p.m. to Pier Head steams out of Ventnor on 9 June 1952, hauled by No. 20 *Shanklin* unusually running chimney-first on an up train.

[Brian Morrison]

An '02' bursts out of the northern end of Ventnor Tunnel with an up train in July 1965. The engine will soon need a visit to shed for coal as the bunker appears to be empty. The Island '02s' had their bunkers enlarged in the early 1930s, increasing the coal capacity to three tons, which was sufficient for most of the rosters which the engines had to undertake. The oval number plate is a survival from Southern Railway days.

[T. P. Cooper]

During the autumn of 1963, considerable repairs were undertaken to the pier at Ryde. The entire superstructure was replaced on the original 80-year-old piles and all traffic had to be suspended for the duration of the work. The Ventnor line trains ran as far as the Esplanade station, but the Cowes traffic terminated at Ryde (St. John's Road). This scene at the latter station shows No. 16 *Ventnor* departing with a Cowes train, while No. 36 *Carisbrooke* waits for the road before setting off to Ventnor, having worked in from Esplanade on 26 September 1963.　　　　　[G. D. King]

A close-up of No. 16 *Ventnor* in No. 3 platform at St. John's Road on 26 August 1965. The engine, built for £1500 in 1892 as L.S.W.R. No. 217, is looking its age, with rust and peeling paint on its smokebox and steam leaking from the air pump. Note the S.E.R. monogram on the station seat. [T. P. Cooper]

The Ryde and Newport Railway's line from Smallbrook Junction to Newport was opened to traffic on 20 December 1875 and eventually became part of the 28-mile Isle of Wight Central Railway in 1887. No. 31 *Chale* pulls away from the 'new' platform at Ashey, 2 miles from Smallbrook Junction on 29 August 1965 with the 2.30 p.m. Ryde to Cowes. This platform was built in 1961 to replace the original which had collapsed due to the continued movement of the clay subsoil on which it was built.

[M. J. Fox]

Black smoke darkens the sky
above Ashey as No. 17
Seaview takes the 10.36 a.m.
from Ryde (Esplanade) on
towards its destination, Cowes,
on 17 February 1966.
[D. T. Cobbe]

No. 17's nameplate in
pre-war days. [C. G. Woodnutt]

A splendid study of a typical Isle of Wight scene in the 'good old days'. A nicely-cleaned No. 14 *Fishbourne* steams off in the rural surroundings at Ashey on 22 August 1965. Apart from the B.R. lined-black livery of the tank, such a scene could be dated at any period from 1923-1967, this being one of the fascinations of the Island's rail services.

[A. E. Bennett]

The summer flowers and ripening grasses frame No. 21 *Sandown* as the 0-4-4 tank coasts towards Haven Street with a train from Ryde, 22 August 1965. The headcode for the Ryde to Cowes services was the two discs above the buffers.

[A. E. Bennett]

Country railwaymen took a great pride in 'their' stations and the Southern sensibly acknowledged the spirit of friendly rivalry among its employees. This prize-winning seat has a place of honour at Haven Street, 1965.

[T. P. Cooper]

Haven Street, five miles from Ryde, was a crossing point; No. 21 *Sandown* waits with an up train as No. 14 *Fishbourne* brakes for the stop at the platform, 22 August 1965.

[A. E. Bennett]

The 150-ton six-coach sets used on certain turns taxed the '02s' to the limit. No. 30 *Shorwell* has been worked hard, as the burnt smokebox door can testify. The engine poses at Haven Street with the 4.30 p.m. Ryde to Cowes, 8 August 1961.

[D. T. Cobbe]

The Maunsell lined-green livery suited the Adams tanks very well, as is seen in this view of No. 28 *Ashey*, appropriately taken at the station of that name in October 1937. The engine is running bunker-first with a down train to Newport. The oval plate on the rear of the bunker carries the number W28 and the words Southern Railway, a title which was chipped off many of the tanks in 1948 in an excess of zeal at the time of Nationalisation.

[C. G. Woodnutt]

The engine number and B.R. emblem have had a wipe over with an oily rag but otherwise No. 24 *Calbourne* looks in a sorry state as it works the 12.36 p.m. Esplanade to Cowes on 19 February 1966. The location is between Haven Street and Wootton, a section which closed to traffic two days later.   [D. T. Cobbe]

With cylinder cocks open, No. 31 *Chale* spins along between Haven Street and Wootton on 29 August 1965.   [A. E. Bennett]

No. 31 *Chale* passes the simple platform at Whippingham, 29 August 1965. The station was built for the exclusive use of Queen Victoria who later agreed to it being opened to the public.

[A. E. Bennett]

No. 16 *Ventnor* passes Wootton station, three miles from Newport on 29 August 1965. The '02s' were designed by William Adams, one of the greatest Locomotive Engineers of Victorian times, who reigned at Nine Elms from 1878 to 1895. Justly famed for his several designs of handsome 4-4-0 express engines, his little '02s', introduced in 1889, outlasted them all and had the distinction of being one of the final classes to run on British metals.

[A. E. Bennett]

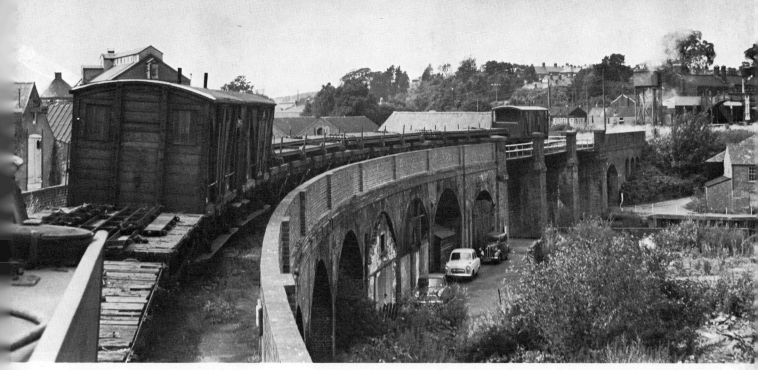

A view from the footplate of No. 31 *Chale* as it heads a permanent way train from Medina Wharf over the Newport Viaduct on 10 August 1966.

[A. E. Bennett]

No. 31 again, this time seen leaving Newport Tunnel with an up train on 29 August 1965.

[A. E. Bennett]

The first railway to operate on the Island ran from Cowes to Newport. The scheme was initially mooted in 1845, but it was not until 16 June 1862 that trains commenced running on the 4½-mile line. The fireman holds out the tablet as No. 16 *Ventnor* leaves Newport for Cowes on 29 August 1965.

[M. J. Fox]

No. 16 returns with the 4.24 p.m. from Cowes and slowly rumbles over the Medina River *en route* to Ryde. The train is crossing the Ryde section of the viaduct which was built in 1875 by Campbell Johnstone and Co. for the Ryde and Newport Railway, while the Sandown section was constructed alongside by Vospers of Gosport for the Isle of Wight (Newport Junction) Railway's Sandown line. The left hand arch is, in fact, a hand-operated drawbridge, the two sections of track sliding on rollers to one side to allow ships to pass upstream. This was a complicated operation as it entailed unbolting the fishplates and disconnecting signal wires before the sections could be moved. In early years it was opened several times daily but as vessels grew larger and moored downstream it became a rare sight to see it opening up. The Sandown section was dismantled in 1963 and the parts used as spares for the Ryde line. The brick viaduct has now gone completely to make way for a new by-pass for Newport. The actual drawbridge span and associated equipment, however, have been 'rescued' by the Isle of Wight County Council and made available to the Wight Locomotive Society.
[M. J. Fox]

No. 32 *Bonchurch* stands at the head of the R.C.T.S. Isle of Wight Rail Tour in Newport station on 18 May 1952. Alongside is No. 3 *Ryde*, one of the four 'E1' 0-6-0Ts which were mainly used for freight traffic on the Island.   [C. G. Woodnutt]

No. 34 *Newport*, working 'head-up' at Newport with a Ryde train on 19 May 1952. The engine is sporting the S.R.'s early version of British Railways livery, the new owner's title spelled out in shaded block capitals on the side tanks.

[C. G. Woodnutt]

No. 24, minus its *Calbourne* nameplates, is running in gently as station pilot at Newport, 2 June 1965. The engine has just received the final general overhaul to be given to a locomotive at Ryde Works. The 48-ton tank looks very smart, but the elaborate and attractive L.N.W.R.-style lining of red, cream and grey has been omitted, which leaves the engine looking somewhat undressed!

[T. P. Cooper]

A well-timed photograph catches the exchange of tablets at Newport with No. 31 *Chale* hauling the 4.30 p.m. Ryde to Cowes on 29 August 1965. The Southern usually provided large loops to enable the men to catch the tablets at reasonable speeds.　　　　　　　　　　　　　　[M. J. Fox]

Tank engine crews were constantly topping up their water supply. The '02s' had a capacity of 800 gallons and as they were hard-worked on the heavily graded Island lines this meant frequent stops at the water columns. The fireman of No. 28 *Ashey* fills up from the 'Hornby' type of water tank at Newport before proceeding on to Cowes, 4 September 1965. The fire devil beneath the tank would be lit in frosty weather to prevent the freezing up of the vital water supply.   [D. M. Cox]

The Southern Railway transferred four Stroudley 'E1' 0-6-0Ts to the Island in 1933 to provide additional power for freight working. These 44-ton tanks, of 1874 vintage, were reboilered by D. Earle Marsh and the I.O.W. engines were fitted with Westinghouse air brake equipment. No. 4 *Wroxall,* the last 'E1' survivor, seen at Newport on 1 May 1958, worked until 1960 on its usual rosters, hauling coal from Medina Wharf. The appearance of the engine has undergone a subtle change by the substitution of a Drummond chimney for the original Stroudley copper-cap.

[J. R. Besley]

No. 35 *Freshwater* drifts into Newport on 20 June 1965 with the 2.30 p.m. Ryde to Cowes, having crossed the viaduct which spans the Medina east of the station. The Sandown line which once ran parallel across the structure had been lifted in 1963.

(M. J. Fox]

The name *Freshwater* was carried by an 'AIX' 0-6-0T numbered first No. 2 and subsequently No. 8 by the Southern Railway. When this 'Terrier' and sister engine No. 13 *Carisbrooke* were returned to the mainland, '02s' Nos. 30181 and 30198 were shipped across to Medina Wharf on the floating crane on 13 April 1949 and they assumed the names from the 'Terriers'.

[A. E. Bennett]

BRITISH RAILWAYS

FRESHWATER

Although designed as passenger engines, the Adams '02s', with their 4 ft. 10 in. wheels could handle light goods trains satisfactorily. No. 30 *Shorwell* hauls the 4.35 p.m. load of coal away from Medina Wharf to Ryde on 8 June 1964.   [M. J. Messenger]

The guard's view of the 9.58 a.m. Newport to Ryde goods, with No. 14 *Fishbourne* at the head as it approaches Newport station on 25 October 1965.   [T. P. Cooper]

A down train rattles over the viaduct which spans the mill pond near Cement Mills Halt, hauled by No. 20 *Shanklin* in 1965. This unadvertised halt, one mile north of Newport station, served the siding that led into the old cement mills which processed the chalk dug from the Great Pan Pit, south of Newport. The mills provided a great deal of revenue in days past, but fell into ruin in the post-war years.

[T. P. Cooper]

'02' No. 29 *Alverstone* crosses the viaduct with the 4.28 p.m. Cowes to Ryde (Pier Head) on Saturday 5 June 1965.   [T. P. Cooper]

Run-down '02' No. 27 *Merstone* struggles up the incline at Medina Wharf with a load of coal, 3 September 1965.

[A E. Bennett]

Medina Wharf was constructed by the Ryde and Newport Railway in 1877 to facilitate the unloading of coal shipped from the mainland. Locomotives and rolling stock arrived and departed at the quay. This 1964 view shows a good tonnage of coal loaded up ready for distribution around the Island.

[T. P. Cooper]

The guard raises his hand for the 'right-away' at Mill Hill, the station at the southern portal of the tunnel at Cowes. No. 27 *Merstone* heads a down train in September 1965.

[T. P. Cooper]

No. 24 *Calbourne* emerges from the 198-yard Mill Hill Tunnel as it heads down the 1 in 145 towards the Cowes terminus on Saturday 28 August 1965.

[T. P. Cooper]

6.30 a.m. on a summer Saturday at Cowes, 31 July 1965. In spite of the early hour, the pressure of the biggest holiday rush of the year is beginning to build up, with every track occupied by stock and locomotives. While the winter traffic on the Island was light, there were tremendous peaks during the summer season which taxed the railway facilities to the full. The number 485 on the rear of the coach refers to the set of coaches; the Southern always grouped its passenger vehicles in these semi-permanent sets.

[T. P. Cooper]

No. 21 *Sandown* rounds the curve into Cowes with a train from Ryde on 19 June 1965. When the line to Newport opened in 1862, seven trains were run daily (Second Class return fare 1s. 2d.), this number rising to 27 each way during Southern Railway days. The number declined to sixteen daily at hourly intervals in the latter years of the line's existence. [M. J. Fox]

The interior of Cowes signalbox in July 1964. Life was hard in manually operated boxes but the signalmen were proud of their work-places and the levers and dials were meticulously polished and burnished. [T. P. Cooper]

No. 21 *Sandown* backs out of Cowes station following its arrival from Ryde on 19 June 1965. The engine is reasonably clean but the crew have given the emblem and nameplate an extra polish for good measure. Cleaning was originally the task of boy entrants to the footplate service, but in later years adult labourers performed this work if they could be found.   [M. J. Fox]

The Isle of Wight (Newport Junction) Railway was incorporated to build a line connecting Newport with Sandown. The 8½ miles from Sandown to Shide was opened on 1 February 1875 and the final connection at Newport was made in June 1879 following the completion of the additional viaduct over the Medina (page 65). This company later formed part of the Isle of Wight Central Railway. No. 31 *Chale* is seen at Newchurch with a train for ¬down *c*.1936.

[C. G. Woodnutt]

A Vauxhall saloon waits at Alverstone level crossing for No. 30 *Shorwell* to pass with its Sandown train, October 1951. [C. G. Woodnutt]

'A1X' 0-6-0T No. 11 *Newport* takes water at Sandown after arrival with a Newport train, 10 August 1934. This engine was the famous L.B.S.C.R. No. 40 *Brighton* which won a Gold Medal at the Paris Exhibition of 1878. In 1902 it was purchased by the I.W.C.R. for £600 and it ran on the Island until 1947, when it returned to the mainland as 2640, where it continued to work until 1963 when it was bought by Butlins. After having been displayed by them at Pwllheli for eight years, an engine returned to the Island in January 1973 on extended loan to the Wight Locomotive Society, where it will be restored to Isle of Wight Central No. 11.

[C. G. Woodnutt]

'E1' 0-6-0T No. 4 *Wroxall* at Sandown after working in with the goods from Newport, 1950. [T. P. Cooper Collection]

The Directors' opening special for the Newport, Godshill and St. Lawrence Railway (later part of the I.W.C.R.) at Newport on 19 July 1897. The special ran from Pier Head to Newport, where it reversed, then on to St. Lawrence where there was an opening ceremony. The gentleman in the top hat is Mr. C. L. Conacher, General Manager of the I.W.C.R. The engine is No. 6, a powerful 40-ton 4-4-0 tank built in 1890 by Black, Hawthorn Ltd. (No. 999) for £1,845. This fine engine, with a boiler pressure of 140 lbs. per sq. in. and 5 ft. 3 in. driving wheels, was the first I.W.C.R. locomotive to be fitted with the Westinghouse air brake which was to become standard on the Island in later years. No. 6 was the only engine of the 4-4-0T wheel arrangement to be taken into Southern stock at Grouping, but it was broken up in 1925 when the '02s' had arrived.   [Lens of Sutton]

'A1' 0-6-0T No. 10 swings along the
I.W.C.R. track towards Ventnor in
pre-Grouping days. The engine is
ex-L.B.S.C.R. No. 69 *Peckham* and
was purchased, after a general
overhaul and repainting at
Brighton Works, for £700 in 1900.
(Loco and General Railway Photos]

The I.W.C.R. extended its line from
St. Lawrence to the new terminus
at Ventnor (West) in 1900. The
station was known as Ventnor
(Town) until 1923.   [T. P. Cooper]

VENTNOR
168 FT. ABOVE SEA LEVEL

'Terrier' No. 10, named *Cowes* by the Southern Railway in 1930, leaves St. Lawrence Tunnel. The engine received its name when it was rebuilt to 'A1X' specification and along with sisters Nos. 11 and 12 was fitted with auto gear for working the Ventnor service.

[Loco and General Railway Photos]

I.W.C.R. No. 9 was the first 'Terrier' to work on the Island, having been purchased from the L.B.S.C.R. for £800 in 1899 (ex No. 75 *Blackwall*). Because of its success, three others were bought by the Central. Seen near St. Lawrence, it was withdrawn from service in 1926.

[Loco and General Railway Photos]

I.W.C.R. No. 5 rattles its four-wheeled stock through the chalk cutting near Ventnor (West) in pre-Grouping days. The lower view shows the 2-4-0 tank on a return journey back to Merstone. This engine, with sister No. 4, was built by Beyer, Peacock Ltd. (No. 1584) for the Ryde and Newport Railway in 1876. The 40-ton locomotive was of standard B.P. design, with 5ft. 0 in. coupled wheels and 140 lbs. per sq. in. boiler pressure, and like most of its type was adorned with a copper-cap chimney and a handsome brass dome which the men polished until it gleamed.

[Loco and General Railway Photos]

0-6-0T No. 10 (as yet unnamed) stands at Ventnor (West) in 1924 or 1925. The set was one of two such formations on the Island and was gangwayed for conductor-guard working. They were of L.C.D.R. origin and arrived on the Island in 1924. They worked on the Ventnor (West) branch as push-pull units from 1928-1938; the body of one of the saloons still survives, complete with seating and interior fittings, as a summer house!

[Lens of Sutton]

Motor-fitted No. 35 *Freshwater* tops up at Ventnor (West) *c.*1952. One coach sufficed for most of the year, with two provided in the holiday season. The line from Merstone was closed on 15 September 1952 and today there is a roadway where the wagons are standing and bungalows occupy the site.

[Lens of Sutton]

One of the two motor-fitted '02s' (Nos. 35 or 36) at Ventnor (West) *c.*1949 with the 'new' two-coach push-pull set. The station house still survives, surrounded now by modern bungalows.

[Lens of Sutton]

A Freshwater train, consisting of four L.B.S.C.R. bogies, stands in the bay at Newport, c.1936. When ready to leave, the train will reverse to the spur in front of the signalbox and then set off for Freshwater on the line passing behind the carriage to the left of the picture. While many 'Terriers' were much-travelled engines, No. 8 *Freshwater* must surely be one of the most adventurous of its class. Built as L.B.S.C.R. No. 46 *Newington* in 1877, it was sold for £500 to the L.S.W.R. in 1903 to work the Lyme Regis branch as No. 734. In 1913 it was sold to the Freshwater, Yarmouth and Newport Railway for £900 and entered Southern stock as No. 2 in 1923. Named and renumbered No. 8 in 1930, it continued to work on the Island until it returned to the mainland in 1949, where it remained in service as No. 32646 until 1963, since which time it has been fully restored and is now on exhibition on Hayling Island.

[Lens of Sutton]

No. 30 *Shorwell* on a Newport to Freshwater train crosses the R.C.T.S. Rail Tour at Ningwood on 18 May 1952. Between Newport and Ningwood a private station at Watchingwell was built for Sir John Stephen Barrington Simeon.

[C. G. Woodnutt]

Trains crossing at Ningwood, on the Freshwater line, in 1927. 'Terrier' No. 3, later No. 13 *Carisbrooke,* arrived on the Island in May 1927, where it served until 1949 when the little engine returned to the mainland to continue working as No. 32677 until its withdrawal in 1959. The train on the left has one of the I.W.C.R.'s two short bogie coaches of 1890 as its rear vehicle.   [Lens of Sutton]

No. 8, seen at Freshwater shortly after Grouping, was considered by many of the old-time enthusiasts to have been the most handsome engine to run on the Island. Supplied by Beyer, Peacock (No. 3942) for £1,950 in 1898, No. 8 was larger than its earlier sisters and was fitted with a more commodious cab for the men, with steam sanding and Westinghouse brake provided. Unfortunately this view shows the engine with a Wheeler & Hurst chimney in place of its original tapered copper-cap, while its brass dome has been painted over. It was to survive in this Southern livery until withdrawal in 1929. Below, One of the ex-I.W.C.R. 'Terriers' arriving at Freshwater with a close-coupled set of Stroudley four-wheelers, c.1927.   [Lens of Sutton]

A 'Terrier' at Freshwater in 1927. The 12-mile line from Newport was opened in 1888 but it was always in financial difficulties and the Southern was most reluctant to operate it at Grouping. Below, The 'Tourist'—the through train from Ventnor—arrives at Freshwater behind No. 33 *Bembridge* in 1953, the last year of the line's working. This train was usually worked from Ventnor (West) to Newport by an 'E1' 0-6-0T (often No. 4 *Wroxall*), then an '02' coupled up to the rear of the train and reversed it away to Freshwater.

[Lens of Sutton]

A rare shot at Newport shed. From left to right are an '02' with Drummond boiler, 'E1' No. 1 *Medina*, 'Terrier' No. 4 *Bembridge* and 'E1' No. 3 *Ryde*. As 'E1s' Nos. 1-3 arrived late in 1932 and a further member to be numbered No. 4 in place of the 'Terrier' arrived early in 1933, the scene is probably around October 1932.

[C. G. Woodnutt]

Newport, April 1967, with a melancholy line of condemned '02s' awaiting their fate.

[T. P. Cooper]

A further view of No. 8
Freshwater, this time by
the coal stage at Newport
shed on 12 October 1936.
In later years, on its
return to the mainland
the little engine was
reunited with one of the
elegant Stroudley
chimneys instead of
the cast iron affair
shown here.
[C. G. Woodnutt]

Yarmouth stands
outside Newport shed
in 1950. At that date the
depot (then coded 71E,
later 70G) had the four
'E1s' and twelve '02s',
Nos. 25-36, on its
strength.
[T. P. Cooper Collection]

An '02' poses for its portrait outside Ryde shed on 28 August 1960. When built at Nine Elms in 1890, No. 28 *Ashey,* then numbered 186 had one of Adams's austere but well-proportioned stovepipe chimneys, and apart from the substitution of the Drummond-pattern chimney and the provision of the Westinghouse equipment, the engine was little changed throughout its 76 years of hard service. The railway certainly has a good return on its original investment of the £1500 cost of the locomotive.

[D. T. Cobbe]

A lineup of '02s' at Ryde in July 1965. The shed, coded 71F and later 70H, supplied steam power for all the services following the closure of Newport shed in 1957.

[T. P. Cooper]

Although covered with grime and with rust showing through the paintwork, the '02s' still retained their dignity to the very end. A group of these grand little engines stand amongst sunlight and shadow inside Ryde shed on 31 December 1966, the last day of steam working on the Island. No. 22 *Brading* will soon disappear, but her memory lingers on.

[D. T. Cobbe]

Hope springs eternal in the human breast. Enthusiasts had restored No. 24 *Calbourne* to something like her former glory by 23 August 1969, when the engine was seen at Freshwater. Since that time the Wight Locomotive Society has completed the restoration of the '02', which has been joined at the Haven Street centre by numerous other exhibits. One of these is the Hawthorn Leslie 0-4-0 saddle tank *Invincible*, which is on permanent loan to the Society following its purchase by a Southampton businessman. Also there are 0-6-0T *Ajax* and 'A1X' 0-6-0T ex-B.R. No. 32640, being restored to Isle of Wight Central No. 11 (see also P. 81A). In addition there are various ex-S.E.C.R. and L.B.S.C.R. carriages and wagons. Amongst the goods rolling stock held are an ex-L.S.W.R. 'Road' Van dating from c.1898, and a Midland Railway hand-operated crane, believed c.1865-70, and which came to the Island as one of the Isle of Wight Central's second-hand 'finds'.

[T. P. Cooper]

The view of Newport as seen through the fireman's spectacle of the restored No. 24 *Calbourne*, December 1970.   [T. P. Cooper]